2013 - PRESENT

Contrary to Rotterdam's 'manic hardcore' reputation - ARTS is a label that claims instead to "push of the boundaries of what is accepted as the norm or the status quo, primarily in the art and cultural realm".

THE ESSENTIALS

I HATE MODELS 'INTERGALACTIC EMOTIONAL BREAKDOWN'
VARIOUS 'ARTS V - FIVE YEARS OF ARTS'

B12 RECORDS

1990 - 1996 / 2007 - 2009

Bespoke outlet for the sound experiments of UK slow techno specialists B12 (Infamix) & associates, exploring the brighter, spacier end of the classic sound palette creating stmospheric soundscapes around clicking 808s.

THE ESSENTIALS

B12 'PRACTOPIA'

B12 'SPACE AGE'

TECHNO IS A DANCE MUSIC GENRE WHICH CAN BE TRACED BACK TO 1981, DETROIT, MICHIGAN. COMBINING THE POST-INDUSTRIAL SOUNDSCAPE OF THE MOTOR CITY WITH A FUTURISTIC VISION, THE GENRE IS BUILT AROUND REPETITIVE 4X4 KICK DRUM PATTERNS, ROBOTIC DRUM MACHINE RHYTHMS AND SYNTHESISED STRINGS, RIFFS AND BASSLINES.

THE SOUND TOOK INSPIRATION FROM PIONEERING ELECTRONIC ACTS LIKE YELLOW MAGIC ORCHESTRA, KRAFTWERK AND GARY NUMAN, THE INTERGALACTIC FUNK OF PARLIAMENT / FUNKADELIC, GIORGIO MORODER'S PROPULSIVE DISCO, AND EARLY PROTO-HOUSE AND ELECTRO TRACKS.

AFTER US IMPORTS LATER REACHED THE REST OF THE WORLD, TECHNO'S POPULARITY EXPLODED IN EUROPE. THRIVING HOMEGROWN SCENES WERE QUICKLY ESTABLISHED ACROSS THE CONTINENT, FROM THE UK TO BELGIUM AND OF COURSE BERLIN, EACH DEVELOPING THEIR OWN DISTINCT TAKE ON THE SOUND.

THIS BOOK SHINES LIGHT ON A BUNCH OF ESSENTIAL TECHNO LABELS, AS WELL AS NEW, DEFUNCT & SLIGHTLY OFF-TILT LEFTFIELD BRANDS WHO DESERVE A SHOUT!

Words
Emily Thomas
& Rob Smith

Editor
Colin Steven

Design
Banana Gun

Publishers
Southside Circulars
& Velocity Press

First edition
May 2023

southsidecirculars.com
velocitypress.uk

VP026

ISBN: 978-1-913231-43-9

THE ICON CATALOGUE
TECHNO
VOL. 1

01. ACACIA LABEL
02. ARTS
03. B12 RECORDS
04. BALKAN VINYL
05. BASIC CHANNEL
06. BONZAI RECORDS
07. BPITCH CONTROL
08. CLERGY
09. CLONE
10. COCOON RECORDINGS
11. CYCLE
12. DJAX-UP-BEATS
13. DRUMCODE
14. FEVER AM
15. FORCE INC
16. H-PRODUCTIONS
17. HAVEN
18. HESSLE AUDIO
19. ILIAN TAPE
20. INTREPID SKIN
21. LENSKE RECORDS
22. METROPLEX
23. MONNOM BLACK
24. NECHTO RECORDS
25. NEIGHBOURHOOD
26. NERVOUS HORIZON
27. NOVAMUTE
28. OSTGUT TON
29. PERC TRAX
30. PLUS 8
31. REPHLEX
32. RETURN TO DISORDER
33. SOMA
34. SUPER RHYTHM TRAX
35. THEORY RECORDINGS
36. TRESOR
37. TRIP RECORDINGS
38. UNDERGROUND RESISTANCE
39. VOAM
40. WERKDISCS

ACACIA

1990 - 1997 / 2007 - 2021

Acacia Records was the imprint of Detroit techno's leading lady, K-Hand. It placed emphasis on the joyous side of the genre, pumping out classic cuts with housey heritage and a positive jackin' acid flavour. Rest in eternal peace, K-Hand!

THE ESSENTIALS

K HAND 'THE CREATOR'

K HAND 'LIVING FOR ANOTHER (SPORATIC ADDICT RMX)'

BALKAN VINYL

2007 - PRESENT

Posthuman's label cover all corners of London's techno specturm. From braindancing IDM to acid cuts courtesy of Luke Vibert and harder more industrial sounds as well.

THE ESSENTIALS

JEROME HILL 'I LOVE ACID 004'

GLOBAL GOON 'EURO JACK'

BASIC CHANNEL

1993 - 1995

Basic Channel invented dub techno. Founders Moritz von Oswald & Mark Ernestus started the label in the 90s in and around Berlin record store Hardwax. Their minimal and dub techno innovations still resonate today!

THE ESSENTIALS

BASIC CHANNEL 'QUADRANT DUB I'
BASIC CHANNEL 'PHYLYPS TRAK'

BONZAI RECORDS

1992 - 2018

Loaded with heavy kicks, Reese basslines and whirring hoovers, Bonzai were key Belgian talent in the new beat movement, giving insight into the weird Belgian techno that birthed hardcore styles from acid house in the early 90s.

THE ESSENTIALS

B.W.P EXPERIMENTS 'SYNAPSYS'

TECHNO JUNKIES 'ENTROPY STEP'

BPITCH

1999 - PRESENT

Founded by Ellen Allien in 1999, Berlin's techno sound is imprinted into all the releases, and launched the career's of techno giants like Modeselektor, Apparat & Paul Kalkbrenner. Allien is an often unsung techno hero.

THE ESSENTIALS

ELLEN ALLIEN 'STADTKIND'

PAUL & FRTIZ KALKBRENNER 'SKY AND SAND'

CLERGY

2014 - PRESENT

Cleric, one of Manchester's finest, knows how to roll out wonky UK techno and his label has recently focused on releasing raw, updated psychedelic takes on the hardgroove/tribal sound that chuff along at higher tempos.

THE ESSENTIALS

ALBERT ZHIRNOV 'PANZERTRAIN'

CLERIC '2ND LIMIT'

CLONE

1992 - PRESENT

Despite Rotterdam's reputation for rougher styles like gabber and hardcore, its iconic Clone record store also runs an in-house techno label issuing steady 808-centric releases from respected artists from all corners of the techno world!

THE ESSENTIALS

DUPLEX 'LATE NIGHT CYCLING'

COSMIC FORCE 'TEKNO COP'

COCOON

2000 - PRESENT

A haven for the brighter, trancier and more uplifting end of techno, Cocoon is the venture of iconic techno showman Sven Vath. Vath's personal releases loom large over the label's catalogue: Mystic Voices is a perfect intro to the label's Ibiza-friendly, maximalist approach to big-room techno.

THE ESSENTIALS

SVEN VATH 'MYSTIC VOICES'
BUTCH 'COUNTACH (KÖLSH REMIX)'

1997 - 2001 / 2001 - 2005

Swedish techno wizard Samuel L Session's Cycle imprint, which morphed into SLS Recordings in 2001. Both labels are known for their galloping samba-esque tribal techno sound.

THE ESSENTIALS

SAMUEL L SESSIONS 'THE CORE E.P'
THE SAMUEL L SESSIONS 'TRIBE CUTZ (SAMMY L'S MIX)'

DJAX-UP-BEATS

1988 - PRESENT

Saskia Sledgers (aka Miss Djax) knew exactly what she was doing with this one. Founded in 1989, Djax Up-Beats releases are a masterclass in techno, acid and trance from Europe & across the Atlantic. The back catalogue will keep you busy for a few days!

THE ESSENTIALS

MISS DJAX 'SALVATION'

RANDOM XS 'GIVE YOUR BODY'

DRUMCODE

1996 - PRESENT

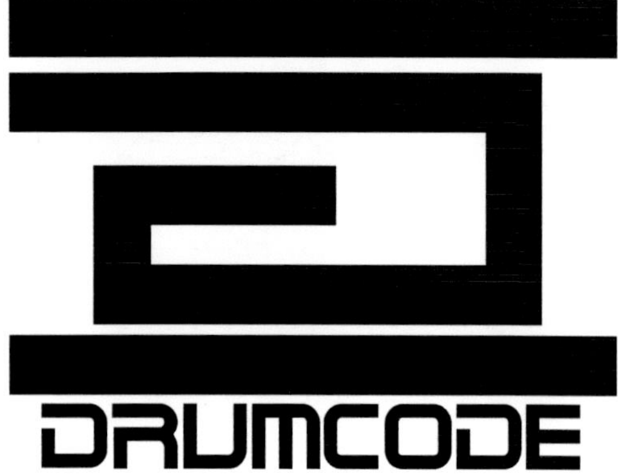

Brainchild of techno giant Adam Beyer, Drumcode has grown from its underground roots to become one of the world's biggest institutions of electronic music. Kickstarting the careers of techno pioneers worldwide and helping push the sound to a global scale!

THE ESSENTIALS

ENRICO SANGIULIANO 'ASTRAL PROJECTION'
CHARLOTTE DE WITTE 'REMEMBER'

FEVER AM

2017 - PRESENT

Founded by a meeting of minds; Mor Elian & Rhyw's label is a beacon of contemporary, boundary-pushing sound design that blends techno with any genre they see fit. Every release is pure gold!

THE ESSENTIALS

PARIAH 'SQUISHY WINDOWS'

RHYW 'BIGGEST BULLY'

FORCE INC.

1991 - PRESENT

Born out of Frankfurt's vibrant techno scene in 1991, Force Inc. champions techno escapism. Tracks from the likes of Ian Pooley, Wolfgang Voight and Space Cube are a crucial place to start if you're keen for a history lesson!

THE ESSENTIALS

PARADROID 'TECHNOLOGY DREAM WAS DESTROYED'
DJ RUSH 'POP LOCK'

H-PRODUCTIONS

1986 - PRESENT

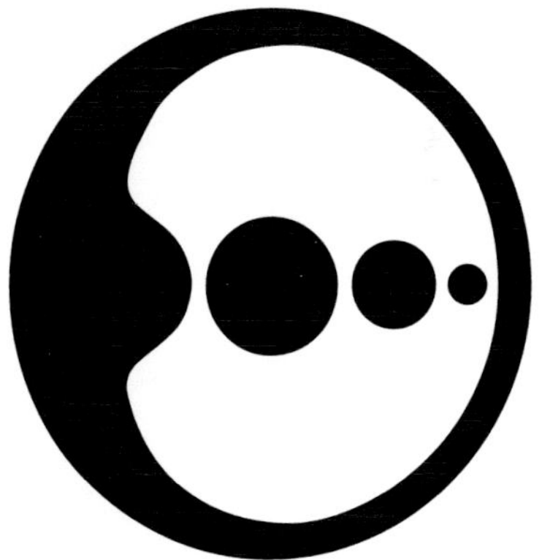

One of europe's longest-running techno labels, H[Hybrid]-Productions is based in Stockholm. Interested in both hybrid sounds and timeless techno tropes, H release club tracks that consistently toe the line between forward-looking and functional.

THE ESSENTIALS

UNDERGROUND POETRY & CARI LEKEBUSCH 'MAD POET'

ADAM BEYER & HENRIK B 'TWO B 30'

HAVEN

2018 - PRESENT

HAVEN

Haven was originally a club night started in Aotearoa/NZ, before moving to Berlin and growing into a goliath techno label. The imprint churns out big room stomp from owners Jaded Nineties Raver and Keepsakes plus the likes of Peder Mannerfeld and Irish techno prodigy Tommy Holohan.

THE ESSENTIALS

PEDER MANNERFELD 'STOCKHOLM SHUFFLE'
KEEPSAKES 'MALIGNANT NOTION'

HESSLE AUDIO

2007 - PRESENT

Born in Leeds by Ben UFO, Pangaea & Pearson Sounds' feelings of dislocation from the dubstep scene. Hessle Audio has since embraced techno, house & breakbeat, resulting in a UK leftfield take on techno.

THE ESSENTIALS

EL-B 'DANCEHALL EP'

GHOST 'WE AINT PLAYIN'

ILIAN TAPE

2007 - PRESENT

Founded by the Zenker Brothers - releasing stoned / wonky / bass-driven techno. Alongside label staple Skee Mask, they've built a repuation as a label more interested in chopped-up tracks with a distinctly cool, moody & texured feel than peak-time shellers.

THE ESSENTIALS

STENNY 'BLIND CORNERS'

SKEE MASK '50 EURO TO BREAK BOOST'

INTREPID SKIN

2018 - PRESENT

INTREPID SKIN

The personal vinyl-specific imprint of one of the most outrageous names in techno, SPFDJ. Intrepid Skin is a dungeon of fast, hard and dirty cuts from current techno icons like VTSS, Shacke & Marcus L.

THE ESSENTIALS

VTSS 'SELF WILL'

SCHAKE 'HARD FEELINGS'

LENSKE

2018 - PRESENT

Lenske owner Amelie Lens has been described by Clash magazine as the 'Unstoppable Queen of Techno'. Needless to say, Lenske has gone from strength to strength since it launched in 2018. If you're looking for big room techno, this roster is the place to find it.

THE ESSENTIALS

AIROD & AMELIE LENS 'JOIN US'

FARRAGO 'HIDDEN POWER'

METROPLEX

1985 - PRESENT

Founded by techno godfather Juan Atkins (aka Model 5000), standing alongside Transmat & KMS as one of the most groundbreaking labels to date. Releases from Atkins, Anthony "Shake" Shakir & Eddie Fowlkes, the label's catalogue is packed with Detroit techno classics.

THE ESSENTIALS

MODEL 500 'NO UFOS'

PLURAL 'SHIFTING FORWARD'

MONNOM BLACK

2013 - PRESENT

Even for Berlin, releases on Monom Black are dark & hard. Dax J's doom-ridden imprint has been a platform for all sorts of evil sonics being created in the German capital, his own track 'Oppressor' gives an idea of the weighty claustrophobic feel most label releases create.

THE ESSENTIALS

DAX J 'OPPRESSOR'

TOMMY HOLOHAN 'INTER DIMENSIONAL HARDCORE BUSINESS'

NECHTO

2019 - PRESENT

The label of Nastia, Ukraine's most famous DJ, literally meaning 'something else'. Nechto is all about championing rising techno artists and raw 90s sounds. Putting out good quality techno music for the DJs.

THE ESSENTIALS

R.M.K 'CONNECT'

LINDSEY HERBERT 'LUCID'

NEIGHBOURHOOD

2016 - PRESENT

Originally a London based party, now consistent label from TASHA. Forward-facing techno, existing outside of the techno purism bubble with tracks like 'Pyramid' showing how innovative the genre can be.

THE ESSENTIALS

RANDOMER & CADANS 'PYRAMID'

FOREST DRIVE WEST 'UN'

NERVOUS HORIZON

2015 - PRESENT

An outpost of innavotive techno looking beyond the 4/4, this London label started by Wallwork & TVSI and focuses on swung, broken techno drawing heavily on middle-eastern samples & dancehall rhythyms.

THE ESSENTIALS

TVSI 'WHIRL'

OBJECT BLUE & TVSI 'TURING MACHINE'

NOVAMUTE

1992 - 2008 / 2017 - PRESENT

Mute Records offshoot Novamute has released heaters from the likes of techno veterans Richie Hawtin, Luke Slater & Speedy J. Relaunched by Daniel Miller in 2017, Novamute's legacy continues with releases from Nicolas Bougaïeff, Terence Fixmer & Charlotte de Witte...

THE ESSENTIALS

LUKE SLATER 'LOVE'

CHARLOTTE DE WITTE 'KUDA'

OSTGUT TON

2005 - 2021

The infamous Berghain's record label was home to some of the best records techno had to offer. Prior to its closure in 2021, releases from the likes of Ben Klock, Marcel Dettmann, JASSS & Barker ensured its place as a dominant force in dance music worldwide.

THE ESSENTIALS

BEN KLOCK - SUBZERO

BARKER - MODES OF WELLBEING

PERC TRAX

2004 - PRESENT

Releasing sizzling techno and experimental electronics for over two decades, Perc's eponymous label is an institution of British techno. Most of the catalogue rich in seething distortion & brutal drumwork.

THE ESSENTIALS

MANNI DEE 'LONDON ISN'T ENGLAND (ANSOME REMIX)'
PERC & PASSARELLA DEATH SQUAD 'TEMPERATURE'S RISING'

PLUS 8

1990 - PRESENT

Created by Canadian techno giants Richie Hawtin & John Acquaviva, Plus 8 has never been the kind of label to follow trends. The label has been instrumental in forging a path for the underground scene!

THE ESSENTIALS

ALEX UNDER 'EL ACCENTUO'

RICHIE HAWTIN & CYBERSONIK 'BACKLASH'

REPHLEX

1991 - 2014

A pioneering experimental techno label founded in 1991 by Richard D. James (aka Aphex Twin) & Grant Wilston-Claridge. Without a doubt, Rephlex left a permanent mark on the techno scene worldwide!

THE ESSENTIALS

U-ZIQ 'TWANGLE FRENT'

AFX 'ANALOGUE BUBBLEBATH'

RETURN TO DISORDER

2015 - PRESENT

Helena Hauff is one of the most revered names in techno. It's no surprise then that her record label consistenly releases master cuts that meld techno, electro and psych rock together as one.

THE ESSENTIALS

MORAH 'TAKE ALL'

DECEMBER '64 WAYS TO ROB A FRIEND'

SOMA

1991 - PRESENT

Owned by Scottish techno wizards Slam, alongside Dave Clarke - Soma Records released the original vinyl version of Daft Punk's 'Da Funk!'. Today, it's still the home of essential techno bangers and shows no sign of stopping.

THE ESSENTIALS

REBEKAH 'CODE BLACK (SLAM REMIX)'

CLOUDS 'DUKE STREET FLEET'

SUPER RHYTHM TRAX

2014 - PRESENT

Super Rhythm Trax is a label inspired by London techno legend Jerome Hill's love of wistful sounds of the early 90s. Ravey pads, squeaky acid, manic drum machines & even the occasional break.

THE ESSENTIALS

LUCA LOZANO 'OUTER SPACE'

JEROME HILL 'IT'S TIME FOR THE'

THEORY

1997 - PRESENT

theory

Theory Recordings is the brainchild of British techno veteran Ben Simms. While releases on Theory and all its sub-labels have explored various corners of techno, Simm's own Vertigo is a great sonic starting point to the catalogue.

THE ESSENTIALS

BEN SIMMS 'VERTIGO (HARDGROOVE MIX)'
REEKO 'AGILE MOVEMENTS'

TRESOR

1991 - PRESENT

Tresor has played a huge role in changing the techno landscape over the last 30 years. Taking its name from their nightclub set up in an underground vault after the fall of the Berlin Wall. With releases from Cristian Vogel, Robert Hood, Jeff Mills as well as new faces like Tygapaw, Yazzus & LSDXOXO.

THE ESSENTIALS

YAZZUS 'METRO CITY BAY AREA'

ROBERT HOOD 'MULTPLE SILENCE'

2014 - PRESENT

Founded by dentist turned DJ Nina Kravitz. Trip made hard and heavy popular again after the dominance of more minimal styles in the early 00s, as well as creating a global platform for Russian artists.

THE ESSENTIALS

VLADIMIR DUBYSHKIN 'LADY OF THE NIGHT'

BJARKI 'I WANNA GO BANG'

UNDERGROUND RESISTANCE

1989 - PRESENT

Since 1989, seminal Detroit techno label U.R. has called for a sonic revolution! Formed by "Mad" Mike Banks, Jeff Mills & Robert Hood, U.R. still releases heaters that continue their original legacy as one of techno's most radical labels.

THE ESSENTIALS

UNDERGROUND RESISTANCE 'THE FINAL FRONTIER'
UNDERGROUND RESISTANCE 'TIMELINE'

VOAM

2019 - PRESENT

As you'd expect from a label co-run by techno bruiser Blawann and ex-dubstepper Pariah, VOAM's releases strike a keen balance between gruff industrial snarl and shimmering psychedelic sound design.

THE ESSENTIALS

RHYW 'HONEY BADGER'

KARENN 'MUSIC SOUNDS BETTER WITH SHOES'

WERKDISCS

2004 - 2015

Werkdics was a well-known home for some of Helena Hauff's heftiest releases, originally founded by Actress for both club tracks & leftfield sounds - it was eventually taken over and phased out by Ninja Tune. However an essential landmark in the UK's techno scene.

THE ESSENTIALS

HELENA HAUFF 'ACTO REACTIO'

ACTRESS 'HAZYVILLE'

SOUTHSIDECIRCULARS.COM